A Complete Understanding of the Groceries Supply Code of Practice (GSCOP)

by Darren A. Smith

Contents of A Complete Understanding of the Grocery Supply Code of Practice (GSCOP)

Introduction

The Annual Survey of 2015 by the Groceries Code Adjudicator stated that 76% of direct Suppliers had a 'fair to unaware' understanding of the Code. This book was written to significantly reduce that number. To achieve that, if you think the book has helped you, please share it with others. You can find how at the back of this book.

Why an egg?

An egg balanced on the edge of a table seemed appropriate as a metaphor for the Grocery industry, Suppliers & their Supermarkets, and for GSCOP. I'll explain why.

The Grocery Industry is facing one of the toughest challenges it has ever had. In the past decade we've seen discounters arrive and begin to make their presence very known, consolidation, large chunks of real estate bought & sold, buyers & account managers wrestling with working in new ways, new legislation, the appointment of a 'tsar', and Tesco has undergone some changes few thought would ever happen.

The egg metaphor also applies for Suppliers who can often feel on the edge of losing their business, winning huge amounts of business, and sometimes that's only about which way they look – Across the table or over the edge of the table.

For GSCOP the egg seems appropriate because in this book you'll come to understand that GSCOP is only a piece of what we need to know. GSCOP is the yolk, the Order is the white of the egg, and the shell was the Bill that was passed. And if we take the metaphor too far, maybe Parliament was the chicken that birthed it all!

The purposes of this book

This book cannot replace a training day in GSCOP, if that day combines GSCOP knowledge with negotiation & influencing skills. The book can replace a training day of understanding GSCOP. The difference being that to understand GSCOP is one thing and this book will help you achieve that objective. To use GSCOP as part of a negotiation, an opportunity to influence, a means to persuade – Yes. This book has been written to help you understand GSCOP. It has not been written as a manual for negotiating better, influencing more, or persuading effectively. Training courses are perfect for honing those skills. To use the knowledge of GSCOP effectively I recommend combining this knowledge with training. And I know the perfect training provider – www.makingbusinessmatter.co.uk

In the book you'll notice a number of (Link). You can access videos, research legislation, and interviews talked about in the book by going to this page:
http://www.makingbusinessmatter.co.uk/gscop-printed-book-links/

Using this book effectively

I cannot over emphasise the importance of understanding the 'rules of the game' because up until now we have been lucky to trade in millions of pounds with nothing but experience, good luck, and a keen eye. To be successful in this new world we need to know the rules and those rules cannot be understood in a few minutes because the rules have 'degrees of grey'.

My suggestion is to appreciate the history of where GSCOP has come from because you need to know why we are where we are. Then read the 'Just tell what I need to know' chapter 2. After which, I hope that those two chapters will have raised you to the next level in the 4 steps of learning – 'I know what I don't know', which will motivate you to move to find out.

GCA challenges Suppliers to understand the Code

The Groceries Code Adjudicator has challenged Suppliers to understand the Code. In this 3.5-minute (Link) video Christine Tacon speaks to Suppliers about why they should understand the Code and says, 'There's really no excuse why Suppliers haven't got to grips with what the Code'.

An image from the Video by Christine Tacon,
Groceries Code Adjudicator

In an interview with Supply Management (Link) Christine challenged Suppliers again:

"We have occasional things come into our office, particularly if a retailer starts doing something we might have a flurry of four or five on an issue. We might have a Supplier ringing us up saying, "this has just happened, is that a breach of the Code?". But mostly, I am goading Suppliers by saying "you have a duty, you campaigned for me for this office to be set up. I will be reviewed in March 2016. If the review sees me to be ineffective we will be withdrawn".

Suppliers tell me the mere fact I exist is making a difference. So when I go out, I obviously make it my business. I am there to hear what they are talking about. I say to Suppliers, 'when I issue my annual survey, you have a duty to fill that in' (Link). That is how I know if things are improving, where the problems are and if I am working on the right ones. They will receive a league table out of it. The retailers care where they are on that league table. So if you aren't prepared to tell me, fill in that survey".

Infographic produced by the Groceries Code Adjudicator's Office

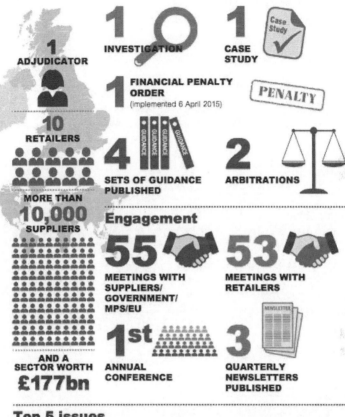

1 ADJUDICATOR

1 INVESTIGATION

1 CASE STUDY

1 FINANCIAL PENALTY ORDER (implemented 6 April 2015)

PENALTY

10 RETAILERS

4 SETS OF GUIDANCE PUBLISHED

2 ARBITRATIONS

MORE THAN 10,000 SUPPLIERS

Engagement

55 MEETINGS WITH SUPPLIERS/ GOVERNMENT/ MPS/EU

53 MEETINGS WITH RETAILERS

AND A SECTOR WORTH £177bn

1st ANNUAL CONFERENCE

3 QUARTERLY NEWSLETTERS PUBLISHED

Top 5 issues

NEW	NEW	CLOSED	CLOSED	LIVE	LIVE	LIVE
Consumer complaints	Delays in payment	Forensics: third party audits	Drop and drive – delivery performance	Forecasting/ service levels	Request for lump sums	Packaging and design charges

Image from the Groceries Code Adjudicator Annual Report and Accounts 2014 - 2015

1. Advice from the Major Supermarkets for Their Suppliers

Each major UK Supermarket was informed about the launch of this book and invited to share their advice for their Suppliers.

Your supply agreement
We've listened to your feedback, and simplified the documentation we use to record our supply agreements. If you lose your supply agreement, just ask your buyer to send it to you again.

Working with us
You can raise any problems you have in the course of our relationship through our Supplier Helpline. The Helpline sits alongside our Supplier Network, which gives suppliers a platform to communicate with us and each other, and address common challenges

Raising issues
We invite you to discuss any queries with your buyer in the first instance. It's important to have an open and honest trading relationship, and the buyer is usually the best-placed person to resolve day-to-day questions.

Need a quick resolution? Contact our Supplier Helpline with your queries – from struggling to contact your buyer to long-standing invoice disputes. You can call us on 01992 806 444, or email suppliersupport.product@uk.tesco.com We aim to resolve any issues raised by you within 48 hours.

We also welcome you to our online Supplier Network (www.tescosuppliernetwork.com). The Supplier Network gives you a platform to communicate with us and other suppliers, and address common challenges.

We take our GSCOP obligations very seriously, which is why we've made it easy for you to raise any concerns you may have.

If you have any GSCOP concerns, you can always raise them with Tesco's Code Compliance Officer (CCO). Our CCO is David Ward, and he can be emailed GSCOP@uk.tesco.com

You can raise issues in complete confidence using our 'Supplier Protector Line' – remain anonymous, if you wish. All queries are handled by an external company. Just email protector@expolink.co.uk , or call on 0800 374 199.

MORRISONS

"It's important that Suppliers know their rights under the Groceries Code and are prepared to discuss them with the retailer they work with. Ideally, this should be their Buyer, but if there's a genuine dispute ask to speak to the Senior Buyer. If you're still not satisfied there's always the Code Compliance Officer. The CCO, doesn't work in Trading and is really only interested in trying to resolve any issue where they can. You can find all the CCO's details on the Grocery Code Adjudicator's web site.

Don't use the Code as a 'negotiation tool'. It's not a substitute for agreeing commercial terms or something to wave in front of a Buyer to try to drive a better deal. The Code is the law, but it's not always clear how it should be applied or how it relates to your supply terms. One simple pointer; it's in everyone's interest to make sure the detail of what is agreed for any supply agreement is clearly set out in writing at the start so that both parties can refer to this if there is disagreement at any point in the future."

Steven Butts, Head of Corporate Responsibility and GSCOP Code Compliance Officer for Wm Morrison Supermarkets PLC.

"Here at Iceland, communication and simplicity are our renewed focus. At our October 2015 Supplier Conference, our Chief Executive, Malcolm Walker, set out Iceland's commitment to be the best food retailer for Suppliers to deal with. This means:

- Quick decisions and quick responses;
- Straight dealing, no strings, no complexities;
- Dealing with stock issues together, fairly. If we've formally committed to a volume in a specific period of time, then we will take that volume in the specified period – guaranteed;
- No consumer complaints charges;
- No listing fees;

- No origination or artwork charges for own-label products;
- Prompt payment, always in accordance with agreed payment terms; and
- 13 weeks' notice before we de-list a product.

In return, we have asked for one thing from Suppliers: simplicity in pricing. We want to sell our customers' favourite brands at an every-day low price all year round. We are bombarded with promotions: half price, 50% extra free, BOGOFs and so on. There has been a massive proliferation of marketing monies, discounts, over-riders and lump sum payments that mean we need a first-class maths degree to work out the Supplier's cost price. These cause both of us a massive amount of time and cost to administer. We want a net - net price; simple, easy and manageable from both sides."

Nigel Broadhurst, Buying Director, Iceland.

The co-operative

"The Co-operative takes it obligations under GSCOP seriously and fully supports the Grocery Code Adjudicator's office. Training is given to both the buying team and support teams that interact with Suppliers to ensure that everyone in the organisation is aware of the requirements of the Code. The Co-operative is keen to have collaborative relationships with its Suppliers and encourages Suppliers to raise any issues they may have at an early stage so we can work together to resolve them."

Phil Willsmer, Code Compliance Officer, The Co-Operative is gscop.compliance@co-operative.coop.

2. Just Tell Me What I need to Know

Collaborating with some friends in the UK Grocery Industry on writing this book, they wanted a chapter on the 'good bits'. The challenge with the Order and the Code is that the devil is in the detail. This chapter is for those people that just want to know the 'good bits' because as I have been told many times by Sales Directors and Account Managers, 'We have the attention span of a gnat'.

The risk is that the devil is in the detail and these are the rules of the game you play in. It's ok not knowing the detail of the offside rule, unless you are a footballer! I urge you to read this chapter and then other chapters to understand the detail.

The 'Good Bits' are that major UK Supermarkets now need to adhere to these rules:

- Ensure the terms of supply are recorded in writing.
- Provide the Supplier with a notice setting out
  its GSCOP obligations, including the identity of the senior buyer.
- Deal fairly and lawfully, applying good faith, without duress and recognising the Supplier's need for certainty.
- Not making supply arrangements retrospective, unless in accordance with specific detailed arrangements in the supply agreement.
- Give reasonable notice to vary supply agreements or to make significant changes to supply chain procedures.
- No delay in making payment.
- Not require payment to marketing costs, unless specifically stated in the supply agreement.

- Not require payment for shrinkage.
- Not require payment for wastage, unless as stated in the supply agreement.
- Not require payment of a listing fee, except in relation to a promotion or for new products.
- Compensate the Supplier for the designated Supermarket's forecasting errors, except as expressly stated in the supply agreement, or where the Supermarket acted with due care and good faith.
- Not insist the Supplier obtains goods, services or property from a third party unless cheaper than the Supplier's source.
- Not require payment for better positioning of goods unless in relation to promotions.
- Not require the Supplier to predominantly fund a promotion. Reasonable notice must be given to the Supplier of a proposed promotion to which the Supplier will contribute. The Supermarket must take due care not to over-order a promotion.
- Not require payment for resolving consumer complaints unless due to Supplier's breach and certain other controls.
- Only de-list the Supplier with reasonable notice and for genuine commercial reasons.
- All of this is supported by obligations on the designated Supermarket to train staff, appoint an in-house compliance officer, and to issue an annual report (a summary of which needs to be included in the designated Supermarket's annual company report).

Action

Please go to the Contents and choose the next Chapter to read. Do you know which Supermarkets are covered by the Code? Do you know if your products are included within the Code? Do you know which Supermarkets are most compliant?

3. A Summary of the history, reason for being, and why you need to know about the Groceries Supply Code of Practice (GSCOP)

In 2001 the Competition Commission made an investigation into the groceries market. The result was to introduce a Code of practice, as part of an Order, to govern the relations between major Supermarkets and their Suppliers. Ultimately this led to the appointment of a Groceries Code Adjudicator in April 2013 to proactively enforce the Code and curb abuses of power. The overall aim of the Order and the Code was and is to protect the consumer (Link) from being over-charged.

The Groceries Supply Code of Practice (GSCOP) is a 7-page document with the intention of providing guidelines as to what fair play looks like between major Supermarkets and their Suppliers. The Groceries Code Adjudicator is the UK's first independent adjudicator to oversee the relationship between major Supermarkets and their Suppliers. The adjudicator has been appointed to ensure that large Supermarkets treat their direct Suppliers lawfully and fairly, investigates complaints and arbitrates in disputes.

Imagine playing 5-a-side football and one player holds another player when he is about to shoot, or a player picks up the ball for a few yards, or the goalie moves the goalposts closer together, you'd want to say, 'Hold on lads, this isn't right'. In the world of Supermarkets and their Suppliers the rules have been mainly written to help supermarkets and for Suppliers. If you don't know what those rules are, how can you call foul play?

Action

Please review the Code (Link), or at least the contents page, to have an appreciation of its contents. I ask this because the Groceries Code Adjudicator believes that we need a new generation of buyers and account managers that work differently. You don't want to be left behind!

4. Where did Groceries Supply Code of Practice (GSCOP) come from? And Why?

The potted history of the Groceries Supply Code of Practice (GSCOP) (Link) is as follows:

- 2001: The Competition Commission conducted an investigation into the groceries market. Following this investigation a Code of Practice was introduced to govern the relations between the major Supermarkets in the UK and their Suppliers, called the, 'Supermarket Code of Practice'.
- 2002 to 2006: The following years after the investigation complaints continued by Suppliers, smaller retailers and commentators that the major UK Supermarkets were using their market dominance to compete unfairly.
- 2006: The Office of Fair Trading referred the UK supply of groceries market to the Competition Commission to investigate and report.
- 2008: The Competition Commission completed a second investigation. The investigation found that whilst the groceries sector was broadly competitive, some retailers were transferring excessive risk and unexpected costs to their direct Suppliers. The impact on Suppliers' willingness to invest in quality and innovation was leading to potential consumer detriment. The result was to recommend a strengthened and extended Code, which should be enforced by an independent ombudsman.
- 2009: The Competition Commission recommended to the government that the ombudsman should become statutory because they had been unable to reach a satisfactory and

voluntary agreement with the Supermarkets on setting up an ombudsman. The Competition Commission made 'The Groceries (Supply Chain Practices) Market Investigation Order', of which the 'Groceries Supply Code of Practice (GSCOP)', was a part.

- 2010: On 4th February the Order came into effect. The Labour Government launched a consultation exercise on making the ombudsman statutory, but this was interrupted by the 2010 General Election. In its Coalition agreement, published in May, the Conservative-Liberal Government announced that it would establish an ombudsman to 'proactively enforce the Groceries Supply Code of Practice (GSCOP) and curb abuses of power'.

- 2011: The Department of Business, Innovation & Skills wrote an 'Impact Assessment' Report (See Chapter 15). The conclusion of that report was that, '…having failed to agree voluntary undertakings to establish a body to monitor and enforce GSCOP, the Competition Commission has recommended that BIS set up such a body'. Following consultation the Government published a draft Bill in May. In July the Business, Innovation and Skills Committee completed scrutiny of the draft Bill, recommending that it should go ahead.

- 2012: In May the Groceries Code Adjudicator Bill was introduced in the House of Lords as one of the first Bills of the 2012/2013 sessions and was first read on 10th May 2012.

- 2013: The Bill received Royal Assent on 25th April and then became the 'Groceries Code Adjudicator Act 2013'. The Groceries Code Adjudicator then began on 25th June. Christine Tacon was appointed as the Independent Groceries Code Adjudicator responsible for enforcing the Groceries Supply Code of Practice (GSCOP), which regulates interactions between the 10 largest Supermarkets with an annual turnover of £1bn and their direct Suppliers.

- 2014: The Competition Commission closed on the 1st of April and all its functions were transferred to the Competition and Markets Authority (CMA).

Action

Please read the above chapter to understand how the Code has been born, and why, because every UK Grocery professional needs to understand why the rules of the game that they are playing in have changed.

5. What is the Groceries Supply Code of Practice (GSCOP)?

It is a set of 'rules' for major Supermarkets and its direct Suppliers to 'play by'. The Code is part of 'The Groceries (Supply Chain Practices) Market Investigation Order', which came into force on 4th February 2010.

The Order is a 19 page document comprising of 5 sections, with the Groceries Supply Code of Practice (GSCOP) being 7 pages within section 5. The full Order is available to download (Link).

Action

Please review the Order, or at least the contents page, to have an appreciation of what is contained within the Order. I recommend this because it affects all Suppliers that supply major Supermarkets in the UK.

The contents page of the 'Groceries (Supply Chain Practices) Market Investigation Order 2009'

COMPETITION 〕〔 COMMISSION

THE GROCERIES (SUPPLY CHAIN PRACTICES) MARKET INVESTIGATION ORDER 2009

Contents

An image of the front cover of the Order from the National Archives

19

The front page of the Groceries Supply Code of Practice (GSCOP)

GOV.UK

Search 🔍

Department
for Business
Innovation & Skills

Groceries Code Adjudicator

See more information about this Guidance

Guidance

Groceries Supply Code of Practice

Published 4 August 2009

Contents

6. What are the highlights from The Groceries (Supply Chain Practices) Market Investigation Order?

- **Part 2** – Section 4 – '…Any retailer with a turnover exceeding £1bn with respect to the retail supply of Groceries in the UK…'. The Order states that all retailers with sales of over £1bn in the UK will have to comply with the Order. The result is that 10 major UK supermarkets are subject to the order (See Chapter 8 for who).
- **Part 2** – Section 6 –
  - 'A designated retailer must ensure that all the terms of any agreement with a Supplier…are recorded in writing…'.
  - 'A designated retailer must not enter into a supply agreement with a Supplier unless the Supplier has a written copy of the supply agreement and all of the terms and conditions…'.
  - 'Written terms of a supply agreement must be held by the designated retailer for a period of 12 months after the relevant supply agreement has expired, or otherwise come to an end'.
  - 'A designated retailer must not enter into a supply agreement unless it has provided…
    - The obligation by the Supplier in relation to marketing costs, wastage, payments, promotions, changes to supply chain procedures and tying…'.
    - …the identity and contact details of the senior buyer…'.
    - …the designated retailer's obligation under the Code to allow a Supplier to escalate a decision of a primary buyer…to the senior buyer for review…'.
    - …the designated retailer's Code Compliance Officer…'.
    - …the identity and contact details of the ombudsman'.

- A mechanism by which the Supplier can feedback to the retailer on the Supplier's relationship…'.
- The procedures for delisting…'.
- The dispute resolution procedure…'.

- **Part 4 – Section 8** – '…A designated retailer must provide to its buying team…a copy of the Code…and train them on the requirements of this Order and this Code'.

- **Part 5 – Section 11-**
  - 'A designated retailer must negotiate in good faith with a Supplier to resolve any dispute arising under the Code'.
  - 'A dispute will arise under the Code when a Supplier informs the Code Compliance Officer that the Supplier believes that the designated retailer has not fulfilled its obligations under the Code…'.
  - 'Whenever a Supplier contacts the Code Compliance Officer regarding an alleged breach of the Code…the Code Compliance Officer will inform the Supplier of their rights to initiate a dispute under article 11 (2)'.
  - 'If any dispute is not resolved by the parties to the satisfaction of the Supplier within 21 days from the date that the dispute arises, then at any time during a period expiring four calendar months, after the dispute arises the designated retailer will submit to an arbitration request…'.
  - 'The arbitration will be administered by the Ombudsman…'.
  - 'All costs of the arbitrator will be borne by the designated retailer…'.

Action

Please get a written supply agreement with your Supermarket that covers the items of marketing costs, wastage, payments, promotions, changes to supply chain procedures and tying. And a copy of their terms and conditions. Plus, find out the contact details of the Code

Compliance Officer at each major Supermarket that you deal with (See Chapter 14 for Code Compliance Officers).

The extract below from the Order shows one of the key principles – A written supply agreement.

Currently only 1 in 2 Suppliers has a written Supply Agreement.

6. Duty to provide information to Suppliers

(1) A Designated Retailer must ensure that all the terms of any agreement with a Supplier for the supply of Groceries for the purpose of resale in the United Kingdom are recorded in writing, as well as any subsequent contractual agreements or arrangements made under or pursuant or in relation to that agreement.

(2) A Designated Retailer must not enter into a Supply Agreement with a Supplier unless the Supplier has a written copy of the Supply Agreement and of all terms and conditions which are intended by the Retailer and the Supplier to be incorporated, but are not fully documented, in the Supply Agreement.

7. What are the highlights from the Groceries Supply Code of Practice (GSCOP)?

In this section we cover the more widely known Groceries Supply Code of Practice (GSCOP), which is a schedule of 7 pages within the Order shown in chapter 5 of this book.

- **Part 2 – Principle of fair dealing**
  - 'A retailer must at all times deal with its Suppliers fairly and lawfully. Fair and lawful dealing will be understood as requiring the retailer to conduct its trading relationships with Suppliers in good faith, without distinction between formal or informal agreements, without duress and in recognition of the Suppliers' need for certainty as regards the risks and costs of trading, particularly in relation to production, delivery and payment issues'.
- **Part 3 – Variation of supply agreements and terms of supply**
  - '...A retailer must not vary any supply agreement retrospectively, and must not request or require that a Supplier consent to retrospective variations on any supply agreement'.
- **Part 4 – Changes to supply chain procedure**
  - 'A retailer must not directly or indirectly require a Supplier to change significantly any aspect of its supply chain procedures during the period of a supply agreement.' (Exceptions apply).
- **Part 5 – No delay in payments**
  - 'A retailer must pay a Supplier for groceries delivered to that retailer's specification in accordance with the relevant supply agreement, and in any case, within a reasonable time after the date of the Supplier's invoice.'

- **Part 6 – No obligation to contribute to marketing costs**
  - – 'Unless provided for in the relevant supply agreement between the retailer and the Supplier, a retailer must not, directly or indirectly, require a Supplier to make any payment towards that retailer's costs of…buyer visits, artwork or packaging design, consumer or market research, the opening or refurbishing of a store, or hospitality for that retailer's staff'.
- **Parts 7 & 8 – No payments for shrinkage…or waste**
  - 'A supply agreement must not include provisions under which a Supplier makes payments to a retailer as compensation for shrinkage…or wastage' (Exceptions apply).
- **Part 9 – Limited circumstances for payments as a condition of being a Supplier**
  - 'A retailer must not directly or indirectly require a Supplier to make a payment as a condition of stocking or listing that Supplier's grocery products…' (Exceptions apply).
- **Part 10 – Compensation for forecasting errors**
  - 'A retailer must fully compensate a Supplier for any cost incurred by that Supplier as a result of any forecasting error…' (Exceptions apply).
- **Part 11 – No tying of third party goods and services for payment**
  - 'A retailer must not directly or indirectly require a Supplier to obtain goods or services, or property from any third party where that retailer obtains a payment for this arrangement from any third party…' (Exceptions apply).
- **Part 12 – No payments for better positioning of goods unless in relation to promotions**
  - – 'A retailer must not directly or indirectly require a Supplier to make a payment in order to secure better positioning or an increase in allocation of shelf space…'.

- **Part 13 – Promotions**
  - – 'A retailer must not directly, or indirectly, require a Supplier predominantly to fund the costs of a promotion'.
- **Part 14 – Due care to be taken when ordering for promotions**
  - 'A retailer must take all due care to ensure that when ordering groceries from a Supplier at a promotional wholesale price, not to over-order…'. This section has been added to GSCOP largely to prevent Supermarkets that might be tempted to order long life goods at lower promotional prices and then continue to sell the lower priced stock after the promotion has ended.
- **Part 15 – No unjustified payment for consumer complaints**
  - '…where any consumer complaint can be resolved in store…the retailer must not require a Supplier to make any payment…', '…where any consumer complaint cannot be resolved in store…the retailer must not directly or indirectly require the Supplier any payment…' (Exceptions apply).
- **Part 16 - Duties in relation to de-listing**
  - 'A retailer may only de-list a Supplier for genuine commercial reasons'. 'Prior to de-listing a Supplier a retailer must … provide reasonable notice…including written reasons…'.
- **Part 17 – Senior Buyer**
  - 'A retailer's senior buyer will, on receipt of a written request from a Supplier, review any decisions made by the retailer in relation to this Code or this Order.

Action

Please ensure that you understand the pieces above and how they apply to you, and your business, so that you know the rules of the game, how to play within the rules and help others to play within the rules too. I advise also understanding the exceptions that apply for those pieces that interest you most. Those exceptions can be read in on this link to the Government's website (Link).

16. Duties in relation to De-listing

(1) A Retailer may only De-list a Supplier for genuine commercial reasons. For the avoidance of doubt, the exercise by the Supplier of its rights under any Supply Agreement (including this Code) or the failure by a Retailer to fulfil its obligations under the Code or this Order will not be a genuine commercial reason to De-list a Supplier.

(2) Prior to De-listing a Supplier, a Retailer must:

- provide Reasonable Notice to the Supplier of the Retailer's decision to De-list, including written reasons for the Retailer's decision. In addition to the elements identified in paragraph 1(1) of this Code, for the purposes of this paragraph 'Reasonable Notice' will include providing the Supplier with sufficient time to have the decision to De-list reviewed using the measures set out in paragraphs 16(2)(b) and 16(2)(c) below;
- inform the Supplier of its right to have the decision reviewed by a Senior Buyer, as described in paragraph 17 of this Code; and
- allow the Supplier to attend an interview with the Retailer's Code Compliance Officer to discuss the decision to De-list the Supplier.

8. What does the Groceries Supply Code of Practice (GSCOP) cover and not cover?

The Order, of which the Code is a part, identifies the major Supermarkets that must comply with the Code and the Order. They are:

Schedule 2

Designated Retailers

Asda Stores Limited, a subsidiary of Wal-Mart Stores Inc
Co-operative Group Limited
Marks & Spencer plc
Wm Morrison Supermarkets plc
J Sainsbury plc
Tesco plc
Waitrose Limited, a subsidiary of John Lewis plc
Aldi Stores Limited
Iceland Foods Limited, a subsidiary of the Big Food Group
Lidi UK GmbH

In the 'Raising an Issue with or providing information to the Groceries Code Adjudicator' form 'Groceries' are defined as:

Included

- Food (other than that sold for consumption in the store)
- Pet food
- Drinks (alcoholic and non-alcoholic, other than that sold for consumption in the store)
- Cleaning products

- Toiletries
- Household goods

Excluded

- Petrol
- Clothing
- DIY products
- Financial services
- Pharmaceuticals
- Newspapers, magazines and books
- Greetings cards
- CDs, DVDs, videos and audio tapes
- Toys
- Plants and flowers
- Perfumes
- Cosmetics
- Electrical appliances
- Kitchen hardware
- Gardening equipment
- Tobacco and tobacco products

In the 'Raising an Issue with or providing information to the Groceries Code Adjudicator' form 'Direct supply is' are defined as:

3. Does the incident concern the DIRECT supply of groceries to one of the retailers listed above? Yes/No

For example, say Jones the pig farmer sells meat to Smith the sausage manufacturer, who then sells the sausages to one of the ten retailers above.

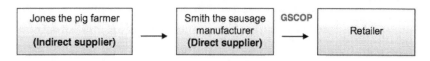

An image from the gov.uk website.

Thus, Smith the sausage manufacturer is a <u>direct</u> supplier to the retailer. Jones the pig farmer is NOT a direct supplier to the retailer.

The Code only covers <u>direct</u> suppliers to the specified retailers. Indirect suppliers are not covered by the Code.

Suppose also that Jones the pig farmer feels he has been mistreated by Smith the sausage maker. That would not be covered by the Code.

It is important to note that the Adjudicator can receive information from anyone – you do not have to be a direct supplier to raise an issue. However, the issue must be about the direct supply agreement with the retailer, not about practices further up the chain.

In the 'Raising an Issue with or providing information to the Groceries Code Adjudicator' form the distinction is made between the Order and the Code. The Independent Groceries Code Adjudicator only deals with breaches made to the Code, not The Order. The Code is a piece within the Order:

4. In your opinion, to which section of the Code does your issue relate?

The Code is contained within a wider Order, known as the Groceries (Supply Chain Practices) Market Investigation Order 2009.

The overall Order is enforced by the Competition and Markets Authority, while the Groceries Code Adjudicator only enforces the Code itself (page 11 and onwards of the linked document above).

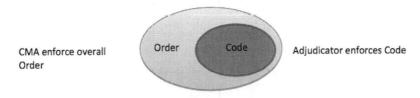

An image courtesy from the gov.uk website.

Action

Please be aware of whether your major Supermarkets are covered by the Order & the Code, whether the products you supply are covered by the Order & and the Code, and whether you are considered to be a direct Supplier. A direct Supplier can be based anywhere in the world. You do not need to be a direct Supplier to raise a breach – The issue you raise must be about the direct supply agreement, not about practices further up the supply chain.

You don't want to score a goal, only to find out it was an own goal. When dealing with legal documents, a potentially complex legal process, and high stakes, we advise that you seek legal counsel. Our partners at Wragge Lawrence Graham & Co (Gowling WLG from mid-January 2016) can help (Link). Contact David Lowe (Link) – Their expert in GSCOP, from a legal perspective, who is very experienced in advising Suppliers on GSCOP. He will provide a free 20-minute email/telephone consultation when you mention this book.

9. Why do I need to care about the Groceries Supply Code of Practice (GSCOP)?

There are 3 reasons why you need to care about the Groceries Supply Code of Practice (GSCOP) and the Order:

1. Being a credible professional in the UK Grocery Industry means that you need to understand what is the right way to do things and the wrong way. Simply observing and copying others is like trying to argue a speeding fine with 'all the others were driving fast too'. Credibility is a key element of the trust model, see below. To be credible you need to understand the 'rules of the game'.
2. A retailer might be asking you to agree to terms that are unlawful. Whilst you will always need to balance your relationship with the commercial realities, you at least need to make an informed decision.
3. Negotiating with a Supermarket Buyer (Link) that has had to be trained in the Code is going to give a buyer the edge. If you do not understand the Code it may weaken your negotiation, if only because 'knowledge is power'.

$$TRUST = \frac{CREDIBILITY + RELIABILITY + INTIMACY}{SELF\ ORIENTATION}$$

Action

Please understand the Trust model and why it can be useful to know the 4 elements that make up trust so that you can improve trust with your Supermarket Buyer (Link) to achieve a win:win.

10. What does the Groceries Supply Code of Practice (GSCOP) mean for Supermarkets and Suppliers?

Speaking negatively about the present

The Code will make buyers more cautious about their decisions because the consequences are greater, and the relationship could become more administrative as each party tries better to cover themselves with 'in writing' agreements. The sad element is that hospitality is much harder to do. Whilst there were always those 'bad apples' that pushed the boundaries too far, being away from work and doing something different, like watching Rugby together, helps to build relationships.

Speaking positively about the present

The Code is an opportunity to re-asses the working relationship and potentially a platform to build a more collaborative, transparent and trustworthy relationship because more items now have to be 'above board' and less is about trading in the shadows. An opportunity to truly embrace Category Management (Link), which aims to build a bigger pie, rather than fighting for a bigger slice of the old pie, by understanding and meeting shoppers' needs better. True Category Management aims to increase profit by identify opportunities to grow, rather than 'fighting' for the same profit.

Speaking about the future

Those people we talk to in the industry about the Code fall into one of 3 camps;

The Cynics – 'Waste of time, nothing will ever change and the Code has no teeth. The only Suppliers that complain are those that have nothing to lose'. The cynics are right in that there have been very few complaints and the test isn't how the Supplier is treated during the arbitration, but whether they meet with an 'accident' later down the line. This is a tough challenge for the GCA because once a Supplier has complained they almost need to be 'looked after for life'.

Certainly the Consumers International body, founded in 1960, comprised of 240 member organisations, across 120 countries, concludes in this paper in 2012 (Link), that the UK is similar to Europe and that effective measures are still urgently needed. Whether they would still think the UK needs more effective measures is unknown.

The Switzerlands – 'I can see the why we need the Code and what it brings, I struggle with whether it's enough'. This group knows that the Code is needed; they also know that it is limited in what in delivers. They're waiting to be convinced one way or the other, either through talking to other professionals in the industry or, by a landmark case, or by a change in the Code.

The Optimists – 'A Code was needed to curb abuses of power. The Code has been strengthened once and now an Adjudicator appointed. These are good signs for Suppliers'. Of course the optimists look for the positive and are seeing real signs that demonstrate change. They are ignoring that these have taken 15 years to achieve. Although the UK seems to be leading the way, ahead of Europe, in managing the situation. The optimists would suggest that what has been done is a good start and long may it continue to grow in strength.

In our opinion

The Order, the Code and the Adjudicator are needed. The principals they suggest are welcomed;

- Achieving Clarity: Striving for clarity so that both parties understand what is expected.

- Proactive   Not dealing with problems retrospectively, Management: but proactively.

- Playing Fairly: Being demanding, being fair, without using sanctions.

We now need a period where the GCA works to gain the trust of the Suppliers so that the 'real picture' can be understood and managed accordingly. For here and now we suggest that Suppliers work transparently with their major Supermarkets by declaring that they understand the Order and the Code.

The best way to use the Code is not to use the Code. Understand the Code. Declare that you know the Code. Work together within the Code. 'Aware and Declare'.

As Steve Butts says in his opening statement, the Code is not a negotiating tool, and we support this perspective. We believe that the Code is to be used to guide Supermarkets and their Suppliers to work more collaboratively together.

We suggest that Suppliers declare that they have an understanding of the Code because this supports an honest, open and direct approach. To achieve this we invite you to become a member of the 'GSCOP Aware Association'. To become a member of gscopaware.co.uk you will need to pass an online assessment. This will prove that you understand the Code and then you'll receive a membership number and the right to the use GSCOP Aware logo on your supermarket presentations and particularly as part of your Joint Business Plan (JBP). Just go to gscopaware.co.uk

Action

Do you have an opinion? Please share it with us by using the comments box beneath this post, or email us at helpme@makingbusinessmatter.co.uk

11. How do I use The Groceries Supply Code of Practice (GSCOP)?

You have read some of the history, read some of the excerpts from the Order and the Code and are thinking, 'How do I use this?'. This question comes from the pragmatist learning style (Link) and is very valid. As professionals in the UK Grocery Industry too, we know that you want a practical guide. Here it is:

Supply Agreements

You should have a supply agreement in writing and a copy of the Supermarket's terms and conditions because then you know what is agreed and is not agreed. A Supermarket can no longer ask you for payments for what has happened retrospectively, e.g. Funding a promotion that has already started.

Action: Respectfully request, or propose, a supply agreement. 56% of suppliers have a written supply agreement and it is a legal requirement for the Supermarket to have this with you. You will struggle to work with the Code if you do not have a written supply agreement.

Supply Chain

The Supermarket can no longer significantly change any part of the supply chain that affects you without giving you reasonable notice, e.g. Asking for an additional delivery day in the week or delivering twice a day to start next week.

Action: Ensure that you and your colleagues in Supply Chain are aware so that you can discuss challenges internally around GSCOP before you reply to the Supermarket.

Payment terms

The Supermarket must pay the invoices according to the written supply agreement. If you have agreed 90-day payment terms then the Supermarket must adhere to this to avoid breaching the Code.

Action: Understand whether you are paid on time and discuss internally if this is an issue that you wish to raise with your Supermarket.

Marketing costs

You cannot be asked for payments towards buyer visits, artwork packaging/design, consumer/market research, store openings/refurbishments, or hospitality, unless these costs are written into the Supply Agreement.

Action: Find out whether any member of you team is agreeing to these payments and then discuss internally whether you wish to raise this issue with the Supermarket.

Shrinkage and Wastage

The Supermarket shall not require the Supplier to make payments for shrinkage or wastage, unless it is caused by Supplier negligence.

Action: Find out whether any member of you team is agreeing to these payments and then discuss internally whether you wish to raise this issue with the Supermarket.

Listings and Positionings

You cannot be asked to pay for listings, or a positioning on a shelf, or to gain more shelf space, unless it is relation to a promotion.

Action: Find out whether any member of you team is agreeing to these payments and then discuss internally whether you wish to raise this issue with the Supermarket.

Compensation for Forecasting Errors

The Supermarket must fully compensate the Supplier for any costs incurred through forecasting errors.

Action: Discuss the last 12 months internally and the potential value of the compensation and then agree whether to raise the issue with your Supermarket.

Third Party Goods and Services

You do not need to obtain goods or services from a company appointed by a Supermarket where the Supermarket receives a payment.

Action: Find out whether any member of you team is agreeing to working with an appointed provider that you know receives payments and then discuss internally whether you wish to raise this issue with the Supermarket.

Promotions

You should not be the predominant funder of a promotion.

Action: Review the last 12 months internally and the potential value of moving from 'predominant' to 'not predominant' and then agree whether to raise the issue with your Supermarket.

Customer Complaints

The Supermarket cannot ask for payment for complaints made by shoppers in store. The Supermarket can ask for payment for complaints that are not resolved in-store, but the watchword is that the payment must be 'reasonable'.

Action: Discuss the last 12 months internally and the potential value of the compensation and then agree whether to raise the issue with your Supermarket.

De-listing a Supplier

You can only be delisted for genuine commercial reasons and reasonable notice must be provided with the reasons for the de-list in writing.

Action: If this is likely for you understand the Code comprehensively for this section and read these guidance notes from the GCA (Link).

Action

The Code came into play almost 15 years ago, has been strengthened to support Suppliers and an adjudicator appointed. Are you aware of exactly what you can and cannot be asked for by major Supermarkets? To use the Code effectively the knowledge of the Code needs to be successfully combined with powerful negotiation skills (Link) and influencing with impact (Link).

12. What was the 2015 Performance Update of the Groceries Supply Code of Practice (GSCOP)?

- Responses doubled from 2014 to 2015.
- 48% of direct Suppliers still have only a fair understanding of the Code. 39% of larger Suppliers have had training on the Code, compared to 32% of medium Suppliers, and only 24% of small Suppliers.
- 8 out of 10 Suppliers stated that they had experienced issues that could be breaches of the Code in the previous 12 months. The main breaches were around variation to the supply agreement, unjustified charges for consumer complaints and an obligation to contribute to market costs.

Buyers' compliance to the Code is still very variable with Iceland being the worst and Aldi being the best

New this year: How well do Buyers comply with the Code?

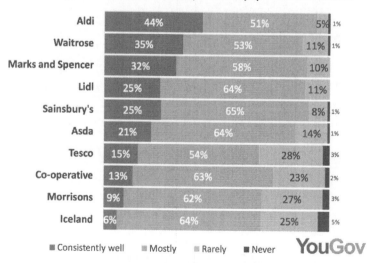

An image from the CGA - Annual Survey Results 2015

- 38% of direct Suppliers said they raise an issue with the GCA, 18% said no, and 44% were unsure. The main reason for not wanting to raise a complaint was 'fear of retribution'.
- Only about half of Suppliers have a written supply agreement.
- Only 40% of Suppliers know who, or how to contact their Code Compliance Officer.
- Most issues were raised against Tesco. None against Waitrose, Aldi, or Lidl – See below.

Raising issues with a retailer in the last year

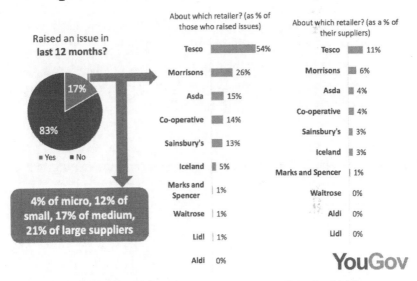

An image from the GCA - Annual Survey Results 2015

Reviewing the published Compliance Reports

The British Brands Group has reviewed the compliance reports (Link) of each Supermarket for five years. They highlight good points about the need for clarity in the Supermarkets' reports. An extract from their 2015 report is shown below:

As can be seen from the summary, Aldi, Iceland and Waitrose provide no information in this area (as opposed to a 'nil return') so it is unclear whether there have been no alleged or actual breaches or they are reluctant to report them.

A marked change this year is that more retailers have been prepared to give actual numbers of alleged breaches, sometimes including how many incidents were raised with the Code Compliance Officer (CCO). Asda, Morrisons, Sainsbury and Tesco have provided this information this year.

Most suppliers are likely to allege breaches direct with retail buyers in the first instance, so the quoted numbers can be expected to be significantly less than the total number of alleged breaches. Of those retailers who report, most use vague language to indicate alleged breaches (eg "a small number"), though Tesco quantifies these.'

Action

You can take part in the survey each year. The announcement will be made on this webpage (Link). The survey for 2015 has now been closed. Please look out for 2016 to be open from about 26th March 2016 to May 2016 and be part of the solution and not part of the problem. You can add the dates to your diary from this key dates webpage (Link).

13. What do I do if I want to raise a dispute against a breach of the Groceries Supply Code of Practice (GSCOP)?

The advice for Suppliers, according to the Order, is to:

1. Negotiate in good faith to resolve the issue directly with your buyer.
2. If the above is not successful raise a dispute with the Code Compliance Officer at the major Supermarket.
3. If the above is not successful within 21 days the Code Compliance Officer must raise an arbitration request within four calendar months, which is administered by the Ombudsman (The GCA's policy on Arbitration – Link - is worth reading).

Alternatively, a Supplier can contact the Groceries Code Adjudicator directly. To do this here are some key files to review:

- Consider what evidence you have using this factsheet (Link).
- Be aware of the process that happens afterwards using this flowchart (Link). The GCA stresses in this flowchart to state that, 'Supplier anonymity is safeguarded'.
- Then, read and complete this 'Raising an Issue with or providing information to the Groceries Code Adjudicator' form (Link).

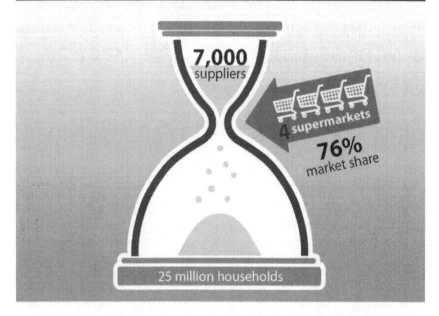

Figure 2: UK - suppliers, supermarkets and consumers

7,000 suppliers

4 supermarkets

76% market share

25 million households

Tania Hurt-Newton

**Image from the Consumers International body paper titled,
'The relationship between Supermarkets and Suppliers:
What are the implications for consumers?'**

Action

Please know how and what it means to raise an issue & a dispute and your rights regarding confidentiality. These can be found in the Bill – Section 18 (Link), which largely guarantees anonymity, though exceptions do apply. Be aware that the GCA can require a Supplier to pay some, or all of the costs of an investigation, if the complaint is without merit or 'vexatious' (To cause annoyance).

14. Who are the Code Compliance Officers at each of the major Supermarkets?

The Annual survey 2015 by the GCA revealed that only 37% of Suppliers know their CCO. The Code Compliance Officers are published on the gov.uk website and can be downloaded (Link).

Meet the Aldi Code Compliance Officer (Link)

Meet the Lidl Code Compliance Officer (Link)

Meet the Waitrose Code Compliance Officer (Link)

Meet the M&S Code Compliance Officer (Link)

Other major Supermarkets are expected to publish their version of meet the Code Compliance Officer in due course. If you are unsure of the name of your CCO, you can review the last minutes of the quarterly GCA and CCO meeting where the attendees are listed (Link).

Action
Please get the contact details of your Code Compliance Officer and introduce yourself. You never know when this might become useful.

15. What were the Highlights of the Groceries Code Adjudicator Impact Assessment Report from 2011?

You may recall from Chapter 4 'Potted History':

*   2011: The Department of Business, Innovation & Skills wrote an 'Impact Assessment' Report. The conclusion of that report was that, '…having failed to agree voluntary undertakings to establish a body to monitor and enforce GSCOP, the Competition Commission has recommended that BIS set up such a body'. Following consultation the Government published a draft Bill in May. In July the Business, Innovation and Skills Committee completed scrutiny of the draft Bill, recommending that it should go ahead.

The Impact Assessment Report was carried out to understand whether to create a Groceries Code Adjudicator. In essence, 'Should a body be set up to enforce the Code?'. The 36 page report is available here on the Parliament website (Link). Whilst it is not critical to know and understand the report, it is useful to understand some of the highlights that led to the Groceries Code Adjudicator being created.

Highlights from the Impact Assessment Report on whether to create the Groceries Code Adjudicator

GCA is part of the Government's Business Plan
The GCA formed part of the Business, Innovation and Skills Business Plan of 2011. It fitted under the heading of 'Priority 9: Protect and Empower Consumers'. The Business Plan is available to read (Link).

Review period has been agreed

A review period was agreed before the GCA was given the go ahead. The review period was agreed as 3 years. On 25th June 2016 the GCA will be reviewed. The risk highlighted in the report is that of the GCA not receiving the complaints that it needs to make changes to be effective.

Statistics used in the Impact Assessment Report

- In 2006, six large Supermarkets (Asda, M&S, Morrisons, Sainsbury's Somerfield and Tesco) informed the Competition Commission that the combined value of their direct purchases from farmers amounted to approximately £295m. This compares to £14.3 billion in total agricultural production annually and £16.7 billion in fresh food sales by those Supermarkets in total.
- In 2009 an estimated £146.3 billion of grocery sales were made through 93,000 grocery stores in the UK.
- Aldi and Lidl were not originally to be included in the scope of the Code. Only 8 large Supermarkets were identified in 2011.
- An econometric analysis showed that the four largest Supermarkets paid, on average, between 4 and 6 per cent less than the mean. By contrast, large wholesalers pay, on average 2 to 3 per cent above the mean.
- A Grant Thornton report (Link) studied the effects of commercial uncertainty on Suppliers and found that only 50% of Suppliers felt highly confident that the sale price would not be reduced by retrospective contributions sought.
- The number of Suppliers in the grocery supply chain was estimated between 2,500 and 10,000 because no known source could estimate the number more accurately.
- Compliance was forecasted to increase from an estimated 68% to 73%.

Action

No action.

16. Who is the Independent Groceries Code Adjudicator and what can they do?

Christine Tacon is the current Independent Grocery Code Adjudicator. Sometimes known as the 'Supermarket Ombudsman'. Appointed as the Adjudicator in 2013 for an initial term of up to five years. Christine has the power to launch investigations into suspected widespread breaches of the Code, including those arising from confidential complaints from any source.

Purpose and deliverables of the GCA

The ultimate goal of the GCA is to promote stronger, more innovative and more efficient groceries market through compliance with the Code, and, as a result, to bring better value to consumers. To help Christine achieve this is the power to impose a fine of up to 1% of the major Supermarket's annual turnover (Link), not just their grocery sales. For Tesco that could be a fine of £690 million!

According to the Draft Groceries Code Adjudicator Bill (Link), which became known as the 'Groceries Code Adjudicator Act 2011', the purpose and deliverables by the GCA are (Page 8):

'17. The sole purpose of the Adjudicator will be to enforce and oversee the Groceries Code in the ways described in the Bill. This will help to remedy some of the imbalance between large retailers and Suppliers, which was reported on by the Competition Commission. The report of the Competition Commission also considered that this would operate in the long term interests of consumers, because the

Groceries Code would help to encourage innovation and investment by Suppliers.'

'18. In order to help deliver these objectives, the Adjudicator established by the Bill will do the following things:

- Arbitrate disputes between large retailers and their direct Suppliers, or appoint another person to do so. This will be part of the dispute resolution scheme provided by the Groceries Supply Order;
- Investigate possible breaches of the Groceries Code by large retailers;
- Where an investigation finds that a large retailer has breached the Groceries Code, decide whether to make recommendations to the retailer, require it to publish information about the investigation or (if the Secretary of State adds a power to do so) impose a financial penalty on the retailer;
- Publish guidance on when and how investigations will proceed and how these enforcement powers will be used;
- Advise large retailers and Suppliers on the Groceries Code; report annually on his or her work and recommend changes to the Groceries Code.

Christine has stated that her top five breaching issues to tackle are:

- Forecasting/Service levels
- Request for lump sum payments
- Packaging and design charges
- Consumer complaints – The GCA has declared this issue resolved (Link).
- Delays in payment

Funding the GCA

The GCA is funded by levies on the top 10 major Supermarkets. These takes two forms; 1. A general levy on major Supermarkets, and 2. Recovery of costs of arbitrations undertaken, and of those investigations where one or more Supermarkets are found to have breached the Code. The current GCA levies are £1.1m covering a modest organisation, unlike other industry regulators, of only 5 staff.

Christine Tacon's background

Christine's background is as a Brand Manager at Mars, Marketing Director of Redland plc, Co-op Farms MD, and is currently also Non
Executive Director of the Met Office, Non Executive Director of Anglia Farmers and several other positions. And was awarded a CBE in 2004.

The GCA online

- Christine Tacon CBE Linkedin profile and website.
- You can hear Christine talk about her role in this 11-minute video.
- Twitter is @UKGCA and use #GSCOP.
- The GCA's Youtube Channel is Youtube.
- Register for the GCA Quarterly Newsletter.
- Register for the gov.uk Groceries Code Adjudicator newsletter.
- See Sketched minutes from the GCA Conference.
- Read minutes from the GCA Meetings with Code Compliance Officers.

GCA workshops for Suppliers

- GCA Design workshop (Link).
- GCA Trade Association (Link).

This webpage (Link) provides the Government's history that led to the establishment of the GCA, Room 2.17, Victoria House, Southampton Row, Holborn, London, WC1B 4DA.

Action

Please keep up-to-date with the issues that Christine is tackling by keeping an eye on this webpage (Link) or creating a Google Alert (Link) for 'Groceries Code Adjudicator' / 'GSCOP' / 'Groceries Supply Code of Practice', or by signing-up to our blog (Link).

17. What can we learn from case studies by the GCA?

The Groceries Code Adjudicator has published 3 case studies (Link) under the heading of 'Code Clarification'. These studies are designed as a means of clarifying the 'grey' to help both the Supermarkets and their Suppliers to know what is right and what is wrong, according to the Code. As with any law it can be open to interpretation and case studies 'kick the tyres' and help us understand what is more clearly meant.

Case Study #1 – Charging for optimum shelf positioning

Overview
This case study looked at Tesco charging Suppliers for better shelf positioning. Possibly contravening paragraph 12 of GSCOP – No payments for positioning of goods unless in relation to promotions.

Key Points
The British Brands Group wrote to the GCA about an article that appeared in the Grocer magazine called, 'Tesco Suppliers asked to pay for eye-level display' (Link). The concern was that this was new practise by Tesco, possibly going against GSCOP, and that incentivising Suppliers, rather than positioning according to what shoppers wanted, is not the future that the GCA wants.

Outcome
The GCA concluded that for a Supermarket to ask for payment for shelf positioning was contrary to the spirit of GSCOP because whilst Suppliers did not have to pay for better shelf positioning, if they did

not, their shelf position would suffer. In an interview with Supply Management Christine added further clarity (Link):

'It is two strikes for one behaviour. So if you take the one on Tesco's shelf positioning, I can't then have an issue with another retailer over shelf positioning. It is a first strike for something I consider to be wrong. Interestingly, the big discussion about the Tesco case study was the buyer had thought it was just a 'request' for payments. But what we said is if you didn't adhere to that request the natural assumption would be you would be put on a worse shelf, so you would be worse-off, there would be a detrimental impact if you hadn't agreed to the request. Therefore, it was a "requirement" not a request.

That case study highlighted the difference between the two. Nobody can come to me now and say, "I thought that was a request, not a requirement"; because I have made it very clear how I rule on that. We are trying to set precedents in our Code so that people can understand things.'

Case Study #2 – Payments for failure to meet target service levels

<u>Overview</u>
This case study looked at Co-op requesting Suppliers to pay for not meeting target service levels. Possibly contravening paragraph 3 of GSCOP – Variation of supply agreement and terms of supply.

<u>Key Points</u>
The GCA was approached by Suppliers who had been asked to make payments for failing to meet targets service levels. The Co-op said that there had been a loss of profit and also did not provide any evidence.

<u>Outcome</u>

The GCA has stated that this practice is not consistent with GSCOP and the practice has been stopped by Co-op.

Case Study #3 – Payments for multi-channel participation

Overview

This case study looked at Morrison's approaching Suppliers requesting support for greater exposure of their products in their convenience and online formats. Possibly contravening paragraph 9 of GSCOP – Limited circumstances for payments as a condition of being a Supplier.

Key points

Morrison's says that it was clear with Suppliers engaged in the selection process that they were requesting monies for support to feature selected products for the online and convenience formats and that it was not a requirement.

Outcome

The GCA concluded 3 points:

- Multi-channel is part of the normal operations, and therefore this request contravened paragraph 9 of GSCOP. For Morrisons to do this they must first agree new supply terms.
- Morrisons had breached the Code because they varied the supply agreements and by making deductions from the trading accounts of 67 Suppliers. Suppliers have now been reimbursed.
- The GCA accepted that the initiative was a request and not a requirement.

Action

Please stay up-to-date on Case Studies so that you can understand which items in the Code the GCA is making the 'grey' of GSCOP more black and white. The GCA will publish their case studies (Link). The update from 2013 also began to provide some clarity on the 'grey' (Link).

18. What was the Tesco investigation by the GCA about?

In February 2015 the Groceries Code Adjudicator, Christine Tacon, launched an investigation into Tesco (Link). The reason was because the GCA had formed reasonable suspicion that the Supermarket had breached GSCOP. The decision was made having considered information relating to the profit statement announced by Tesco in September 2014.

The investigation is likely to take 9 months and will look at the conduct of Tesco from 25th June 2013 to 5th February 2015, concluding in November 2015 and focuses on:

- Delay in payments.
- Payments for better positioning of products on shelf.
- The principle of fair dealing.

The investigation is only with Tesco, though, if evidence comes to light about similar practices from other Supermarkets, the scope of the investigation could be widened. Christine said, "This is the first investigation I have launched and it is a significant step for the GCA. I have taken this decision after careful consideration of all the information submitted to me so far. I have applied the GCA published prioritisation principles to each of the practices under consideration and have evidence that they were not isolated incidents, each involving a number of Suppliers and significant sums of money."

Action

Please stay abreast of the development on the Tesco investigation. If you connect with us on social media we'll keep you informed.

19. Additional reading to help you further understand GSCOP

A handful of GSCOP in the news

- Malcolm Walker: 'Why Iceland is finding a better way of dealing with Suppliers'
- A legal perspective on GSCOP from Wragge Law Firm.
- The Grocer reports on Tesco improvements and Iceland troubles.
  - Food Manufacture talks of 'Tesco admits to Groceries Code breaches'.
- Fruitnet challenges that 'Indirect Suppliers should be included in GSCOP'.
- The Daily Telegraph reported that, 'Tesco and Morrison's receive the lion's share of Supermarket complaints from Suppliers'.
- '7 Key points Suppliers need to know about GSCOP' by Essential Retail.

Associations talking about GSCOP

- NFU: A guide for NFU Members
- The Food and Drink Federation
- The British Brands Group Association provides GSCOP training for 1 day for £500.

Also worth understanding

- The US 'Robinson-Patman' Act aims to prevent large sellers from offering different prices to different buyers where the effect is to harm even a single small firm.

20. GSCOP related useful Supermarket links

Aldi

- Monitoring their Suppliers (Link)

Asda

- Asda share some information about their performance on GSCOP (Link)

Co-Operative

The **co-operative**

- Advice for Suppliers (Link).
- British sourcing GSCOP (Link)
- GSCOP (Link)

Iceland

- 'Finding a better way to deal with suppliers' (Link)
- Corporate responsibility (Link)
- Voted a great place to work 2014 (Link)

Lidl

- Lidl's Code of Conduct with their business partners (Link)

Marks & Spencer

MARKS&
SPENCER

- Responsible sourcing (Link)

Morrisons

MORRISONS

- Morrisons has information about GSCOP on their website (Link)
- Steve Butts, Code Compliance Officer's slides, from the UK Conference (Link)
- Morrison's new Supplier request. (Link)

Sainsbury's

Sainsbury's

- Working in Partnership. (Link)

Tesco

- Dave Lewis launches new 'Code of Conduct for Tesco Staff' – The Grocer. (Link)
- Tesco's Code of conduct guidelines for employees. (Link)

- Tesco talk about their compliance Code training 'Learning Leap 2'. (Link)
- Code of Business Conduct, including GSCOP. (Link)

Waitrose

Waitrose

- The Waitrose Way (Link)

21. An index to find what you need more quickly

22. About the Author

Darren A. Smith spent his first 12 years as a Trading Manager/
Category Manager at one of the big four UK Supermarkets. During this time he managed a number of areas comprising chilled ready meals, cheese, frozen foods, pizza and fresh fruit, and areas of up to £1bn.

Darren then went on to establish Making Business Matter Limited. Over the past 13 years, he and his team have supported Supermarket Suppliers in improving their negotiation skills, category management and time management.

He has written articles for The Grocer, The Grocery Trader, Food Manufacture, Harpers, Fresh Produce Journal, British Frozen Foods Federation, Supply Management, and People Development Magazine.

About Making Business Matter

Making Business Matter (MBM) is a Training Provider to the UK grocery industry specialising in Suppliers to the big four Supermarkets. Their clients want to secure more profitable wins and choose to work with MBM because of their relevant and valuable experience and unique people development method known as Sticky Learning®.

To combine your GSCOP knowledge with powerful negotiating skills, or effective influencing skills, or a ½ day Masterclass. Please contact Darren on 0333 247 2012 or email him on das@makingbusinessmatter.co.uk

You can view more details about Masterclasses

Sharing the Book with your Colleagues

To share the book with your colleagues just click share (Link).

Or

To forward a link to your colleague via email click email (Link).

23. Free Guides to Download

To download the following Free Guides:

The Biggest 8 Mistakes Suppliers Make When Selling to the Big 4 UK Supermarkets

Our Free Guide (Link) for The Biggest 8 Mistakes Suppliers Make When Selling to the Big 4 UK Supermarkets And How to Avoid Them All

Employees Use Very Little of What They Have Learnt

Our Free Guide (Link) Shows You How to Get Employees to Use More of What They Have Learnt

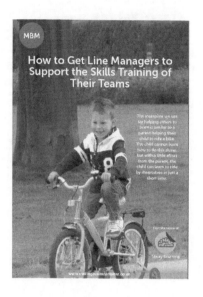

Line Managers Do Not Support the Learning of Their Teams

Our Free Guide (Link) Shows You How to Get Line Managers to Support the Skills Training of Their Teams

Training Evaluations are Rarely Done Well

Our Free Guide (Link) Shows You How to Evaluate Training Quickly and Easily to Understand Your ROI

Keep in Touch with GSCOP developments

Thank You to...

Groceries Code Adjudicator
For their fast responses to my emails.

Major UK Supermarkets
To those major Supermarkets that were proactive and had the foresight to see the book as a vehicle to support Suppliers and one that they could play a positive role in doing so. Thank you for your advice for your Suppliers.

Shapers and readers
Gayle Smith, Andy Palmer of the MBM team, Andy Jenkins, Chris White, Sam Pearl, Alan Chapman, Clive Huntley and Daniel Clark.

Suppliers
To those that were brave enough to tell me when I'd got it wrong as a Buyer, to those that enabled me to see best practise & worst practise, and to many that made my job easier because they truly wanted to understand the Shopper and grow the Category together. To our clients over the last 13 years – Thank you for be willing to work in new ways.

Associations
British Frozen Food Federation and the British Brands Group for discussing the possibility of sharing the book with their members.

Magazines
Ian Quinn of The Grocer and Nina Pullman of the Fresh Produce Journal for collaborating with me on GSCOP articles.

Recommended partners

http://www.supplychainonline.co.uk
Supply Chain Online is the UK's leading Supply Chain, Procurement and Logistics job board. Now in its 10th year, Supply Chain Online provides targeted recruitment advertising to the UK's leading employers.

http://www.wragge-law.com
David Lowe, Partner is willing to offer Suppliers a 20-minute free telephone/email consultation when you mention this book.

http://www.thefreshproduceforum.com
The Fresh Produce Forum powered by RedFox welcomes new members and features news, reviews and debate in all things fresh and agri.

Those people that have tried to sabotage the book before it launched with comments on social media about their GSCOP training course. Thank you because it compelled us to do an even better job because we knew you must be worried! ☺

If you found that your awareness of GSCOP increased by reading this book I'd like to ask you a favour – Would you be kind enough to leave a review of this book on Amazon please? (Link)